TODAY'S YOUNG

SPECIALIST ADVICE FOR AMBITIOUS PLAYERS

CRICKETERS

Shane Warne coaching young cricketers at Lilleshall.

Picture: Gary Prior.

TODAY'S YOUNG

SPECIALIST ADVICE FOR AMBITIOUS PLAYERS

CRICKETERS

KERRY WEDD

Introduction by **COLIN COWDREY**

Contributions from **MICHAEL ATHERTON, DARREN GOUGH,
NASSER HUSSAIN, JACK RUSSELL AND DAVID SHEPHERD**

International photographs and front cover picture by **PHILIP BROWN**

Quiller Press
London

TODAY'S YOUNG CRICKETERS is written to inspire ambitious young players - and all who are interested in trying to help them. The title speaks directly to those already enjoying the game but who are prepared to strive for higher standards. This book offers an up-to-date focus on essential coaching skills, but it also underlines the importance of hard work, of style, of sportsmanship, and of the sheer enjoyment of being part of a united team in search of excellence.

Chapters are headed with specialist advice from top England Test players. There is valuable advice on team-work - both on and off the field - as well as guidance on match preparation, skill learning and fitness. Whether batsman, bowler, wicket-keeper or all-rounder there is plenty for today's young player to grasp. For adults or young players, it brings a clearer understanding of the key qualities needed to climb the cricketing ladder.

A cream colour-code is used throughout the book to indicate more advanced sections.

First Published 1999 by Quiller Press Ltd, 46 Lillie Road, London, SW6 1TN

Copyright 1999 © Kerry Wedd

ISBN 1 899163 55 7 - paperback
ISBN 1 899163 48 4 - cased edition

Designed by Jo Lee
Printed by Colorcraft Ltd. Hong Kong.

CONTENTS

ACKNOWLEDGEMENTS

Colin Cowdrey in action with another majestic off-drive. He scored 22 centuries for England and was recognised throughout World cricket as one of the finest players of his time.

Sales of this book will raise money for The Wheels Fund - to provide several special needs wheelchairs for the young people at The Lord Mayor Treloar School, Alton, Hampshire (see page 71).

I am proud to include an Introduction from The Lord Cowdrey of Tonbridge and to be able to add the support of outstanding England players: Michael Atherton, Darren Gough, Nasser Hussain, Jack Russell, as well as the much respected Test umpire David Shepherd. I am also greatly indebted to Philip Brown (Daily Telegraph) for the use of some outstanding International pictures.

Others I would like to mention: Matthew Clingleffer, John Rogers, Dr Norman Healey and Michael Williams; 3-D Cricket (Glos.) for help with equipment; Alex Fell and various members of Hatherleigh Cricket Club for schoolboy photographs. Jeremy Beswick and Peter Hooper for cricket art work.

I thank them all for contributing to this fund-raising project.

KERRY WEDD

INTRODUCTION

❝ **TODAY'S YOUNG CRICKETERS** *is more than a cricket coaching book.*

Naturally, I hope young players, with their sights set high, will read these words by the author and some of England's finest test cricketers of the day - Michael Atherton, Darren Gough, Nasser Hussain and Jack Russell, as well as from test umpire David Shepherd - read them carefully and then act on them - because this is an action book not just for cricket but for life.

Cricket can - and should - be character building. Through cricket we can grow into better people. This then is not just a volume for young cricketers - though I know I would love to have got my hands on this book as a teenager - the words of these pages and the many splendid photographs are for all cricketers who want to be better players, and for all coaches who seek to produce better, more enjoyable cricket. Cricketers of all ages will enjoy and derive benefit from this specialist advice; whether you are a leg-break bowler, an opening batsman or a wicket-keeper. Every cricketing role, including captaincy, is featured - and all these guidelines are in crystal-clear language which we can readily understand - and yet, at the same time inspire us. Kerry Wedd encourages us to set personal targets.

Ability, concentration and burning desire to improve: the great cricketers have all these three qualities. We cannot all be great players but the author inspires us to become better cricketers - to make the most of our talents. Ability is essential. Some of us are born with it; others work hard to sharpen it.

In general the techniques, outlined so vividly in word, photograph, drawing and diagram, are those which have been employed by the best players over many seasons. Dr W. G. Grace, the father of modern cricket, the man they called "The Champion", who played for Gloucestershire and England more than a hundred years ago, could turn the pages of this book and immediately recognise many of the cricketing principles which worked in his day. Of course, there are

many modern elements too that would have been a revelation for the doctor - sections like fitness and specialist fielding are just two of them - and that is the strength of Kerry Wedd's approach to coaching. He combines the best of old and new.

Though young readers will want to become stronger, better equipped individual cricketers, we must never forget that ours is a team game - on both sides of the boundary - and a match should be played out - fought out - by two elevens with all our combined resources. We should never forget either that cricket at its best is played with a high degree of chivalry. The first edition of the MCC Book of Coaching, published more than forty years ago, touched on this vital character of the game:

"A cricket team should feel that they are playing with, as well as against, their opponents. The home side should remember that they are hosts, the visitors that they are guests, and both should realize that the true greatness of the game lies in combat and comradeship combined."

And there is another side to this particular coin. By buying this book we are not only helping ourselves to become more accomplished - we are helping a very worthwhile cause. Part of the proceeds from this publication go to The Wheels Fund - providing much needed modern facilities for disabled children at The Lord Mayor Treloar School near Alton, Hampshire. It is fitting that cricket can make an important contribution both on and off the field of play. **❞**

Colin Cowdrey

COLIN COWDREY
Oxford University, Kent and England

Legends of yesteryear. Sir Donald Bradman (Australia), Sir Garfield Sobers
(West Indies) and Ian Botham (England).

Picture: Peter Hooper.

YOUR PERSONAL APPROACH

Including • Personal Targets • Check list 1: Personal Assessment • Check list 2: Players' Skills • Check list 3: Personal Equipment • Check list 4: Confidence Check.

66 *This game is all about self-belief - about attitude, temperament and commitment. If you want to be successful in cricket - or in anything else you need to achieve in life - start here. What separates the top liners from the rest is competitive self-assurance - the calm knowledge that*

even on a bad day, you can handle it....We all of us have our highs and our lows - we all have the days when we feel good and everything goes our way - and we all have the others. Those with the wrong approach will probably quit when the going gets tough.

In so many ways, cricket is like life - frequently unfair and often testing - but it also rewards us generously when we least expect it. You need the self-belief - or the inner strength to stay with your game whatever the pressures.

I am lucky enough to have had a wonderful few years in the game. It hasn't always been easy and at times, especially as the England captain and opening batsman, the strange fortunes of the game have tested me almost to the limits. But this is cricket; it is as fascinating as it is unpredictable. If you are the sort of person who will enjoy giving it a real go, both on and off the field of play, I have no hesitation in recommending the game. **99**

MICHAEL ATHERTON
Lancashire and England. Captained his country in 50 Test Matches.

1

PERSONAL TARGETS

TODAY'S YOUNG CRICKETERS contains advice and support from some very experienced players. It is our hope that the following chapters will encourage you to raise your sights - to realise that you can do a great deal to improve your game if you have the right approach.

Most young players reading this passage will already be promising athletes. But which way should you go from here? Is there a sensible way to plan your future…?

What makes you more likely to succeed than most is your willingness to think about how you can improve your game.

When you get down to the bare facts, what have you got to work on? You have your natural ability and your will to learn and to succeed. Most people can live with success - but when things go against you, that's when the first test of character comes and the real battle begins.

One of the most essential qualities for a true sportsman to develop involves this personal battle - this quality which allows you to perform to your best potential under pressure; it includes a refusal to be bowed or beaten without a real scrap; a determination to keep coming back against the odds - to cope positively with injury or disappointment; to believe in yourself when others may doubt. The weak will fade and only the determined will stay with the challenge.

A second vital department involves the way you watch, learn and discover the art of team-work. Even at the highest level of Test cricket there are always lessons to be learned; new ideas to be examined; new ways of doing things. A player with all the promise in the world stands no chance unless he also has the attitude and the temperament to go with it. Equally, the young star who thinks he knows all the answers, who tramples all over his colleagues in a solo bid for individual glory, is heading in the wrong direction.

Make no mistake, good cricket will test you to the limits - but this is precisely why the challenge is so attractive….

Alex Tudor made his international debut for the full England team during the 1998/99 Ashes Tour of Australia. This photograph shows him as a raw 13-year-old, back in 1990. Since then he has worked hard to improve his game. He has been fortunate to have the backing of a helpful family and a strong county coaching set-up in Surrey to guide him – but his progress shows what is possible with the right attitude. Today, he looks capable of becoming one of England's front-line bowlers.

MIKE ATHERTON has already stressed "SELF BELIEF - attitude, temperament and commitment."

Now set yourself some clear targets: try the check lists which follow….

CHECK LIST 1

PERSONAL ASSESSMENT

In the first box, score, on a scale of 1 to 5, how important those factors are to compete at the highest levels.

In the second box, rate yourself, 1 to 5, on this factor.

1 = **Not important**
2 = **Of some value but other factors**
   mean more.
3 = **Quite important**
4 = **Important**
5 = **Very important**

1 = **I am very weak in this area**
2 = **Not so good**
3 = **Not particularly strong/weak**
4 = **I rate quite highly**
5 = **My strong point**

FITNESS REQUIREMENT TO COMPETE AT TOP LEVELS

	BOX: 1	2		1	2
SPEED	☐	☐	ENDURANCE	☐	☐
FLEXIBILITY (suppleness)	☐	☐	STRENGTH	☐	☐
AGILITY (nimbleness)	☐	☐			

MENTAL REQUIREMENTS

CONCENTRATION	☐	☐	MENTAL TOUGHNESS	☐	☐
ALERTNESS	☐	☐	RELAXATION	☐	☐
AMBITION	☐	☐			

OTHER KEY FACTORS

SKILL	☐	☐	TACTICAL AWARENESS (understanding the game plan)	☐	☐
EXPERIENCE	☐	☐	KNOWLEDGE	☐	☐

You can't improve everything at once so make a list of your top priorities. Decide what needs immediate attention and think about how best to progress...Your best move will be to discuss these priorities with a helpful/knowledgeable adult. If possible, share your concerns.

CHECK LIST 2

PLAYER'S SKILLS

When you have checked the sections in this book - and really understand them - tick the box.

FITNESS

Fitness guidelines ☐   Understanding fitness needs ☐   Test yourself ☐

BATTING 8 points of Basic Batting.

i. Equipment check ☐   ii. Grip ☐   iii. Stance ☐
iv. Back lift ☐   v. Footwork ☐   vi. Concentration ☐
vii. Building an innings ☐   viii. Running and calling ☐

Can you demonstrate the following strokes?
Forward defence ☐   Backward defence ☐   Front foot drive ☐
Back foot drive ☐   Pull shot ☐   Hook shot ☐
Square cut ☐   Leg glance ☐   The sweep ☐

BOWLING 10 points of Basic Bowling.

i. Grip ☐   ii. Run up ☐   iii. Line and length ☐
iv. Head on v. side on ☐   v. LBW laws ☐   vi. No ball laws ☐
vii. Close to the stumps ☐ viii. Over the wicket ☐   ix. Follow through ☐
x. Find your own style ☐

Can you explain the grip and action of the following?
Away swing ☐   In swing ☐   Off spin ☐
Leg spin ☐   Googly ☐   Off or leg cutter ☐

WICKET KEEPING 8 key points.

i. Stance ☐   ii. General take ☐   iii. Standing back ☐
iv. Standing up and stumping ☐ v. Leg side take ☐   vi. Fitness ☐
vii. Specialist equipment ☐ viii. Concentration ☐

FIELDING

Long barrier ☐   Attacking the ball ☐   Under hand run-out ☐

CATCHING

Close catching ☐   High catching ☐

CAPTAINCY AND TACTICS

Pre-match ☐   Batting first ☐   Fielding first ☐

CHECK LIST 3

PERSONAL EQUIPMENT

As recommended by the England and Wales Cricket Board.

FOOTWEAR

1. Ensure that your boots or shoes are comfortable.
2. Boots give extra support to the ankles - essential if you are a bowler.
3. Make certain that the metal studs are in good condition. Replace worn ones immediately.
4. Moulded studs or "ripple" sole footwear are not recommended.
5. Wear soft, thick socks to absorb perspiration and to take the "shock" out of hard ground. Two pairs will reduce friction.

TROUSERS and SHIRTS

1. Both items should be loose and comfortable to allow freedom of movement.
2. Trousers with proper fastenings are preferred although nowadays some have elastic fastenings.
3. Wear a vest. It will absorb perspiration and help keep you warm on those days when a cool wind blows.
4. Wear a jock strap with a pouch in which to slip your protector. Wear a pair of pants as well for hygienic reasons.

SWEATERS

1. Both a short sleeve and long sleeve sweater are essential.

HEADWEAR

1. A cap is the most practical. The brim will shade your eyes from glare. Wide brim "floppy" hats serve the same purpose but tend to fly off when chasing the ball.

(*Author's note. Young cricketers will be more confident if given the opportunity to wear a safety helmet. There are sound reasons for wearing such protection - and certain conditions when I make it obligatory - although many players prefer the freedom of a lighter cap.)

BATS, PADS and GLOVES

1. They must be the right size for you NOW. Big leg guards restrict movement and running. Loose gloves mean you cannot grip the bat tightly.
2. Your bat MUST be the correct size and not too heavy. You will score more runs with a small, light bat than with a big heavy one.

CRICKET BALLS

Use a 4 $\frac{3}{4}$ oz. ball until you are 13, then use a full size (5 $\frac{1}{2}$ oz.)

CARE OF EQUIPMENT

1. Always keep your leg guards and boots clean and whitened.
2. Most bats do not require oiling these days, but they must be kept clean and if necessary wiped with a damp cloth. Read the manufacturer's instructions or ask your coach if you are not sure.

(*Author's note. Many young players feel uncomfortable about not lending their equipment to others. Clearly, there are tactful ways of saying "no" but you are advised to keep your own set of gear for your own personal use.)

CHECK LIST 4

THE CONFIDENCE CHART

Any top-line sports person will tell you that self-confidence or self-belief comes right at the top of their list of essentials. You really can help yourself by looking seriously at ways of building confidence. Some call it positive thinking. Study the CONFIDENCE CHART and begin right away to raise your own self esteem. Believe in yourself. Don't be afraid of failure. Raise your sights and go for your goal - and stick at it til you get there!

Learn to think "positive" not "negative".

**Diagram 1
High self-confidence route.**

**Diagram 2
Low self-confidence route.**

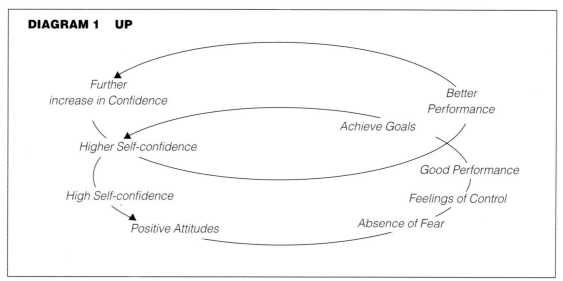

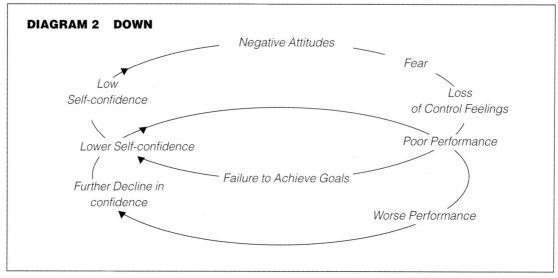

ARE YOU FIT TO PLAY CRICKET?

Including: • A. Fitness Guidelines • B. Understanding Fitness Needs • C. Test Yourself

> *Today's competitive cricket is demanding new levels of fitness - both physical and mental. This chapter is written for young players who are seriously considering how to improve their game.*
>
> *Top-line sports people realise the need for a programme which balances hard physical exercise with the benefits of developing mental strength and a sensible life style. Any player who can learn to take responsibility for part of his own training will be taking an important step towards success…*
>
> *A careful study of the following questions and answers may save you many wasted hours.*

KERRY WEDD and **DR NORMAN HEALEY**

Ian Healy (Australia).

A. GUIDELINES FOR YOUNG PLAYERS

Q1. Do I need special fitness training for cricket?

A. If you are serious about your cricket, you will benefit from a specialist fitness programme. Cricket fitness requirements are not the same as those needed for, say, rugby or football; many of the movements are different. Whatever sport you are involved with, you need a thorough warm up and a gentle stretching programme every time you train or practise. It will be sensible to consult an expert to help provide a balanced programme which takes into account all the games you play…

Your reasons for special fitness training are:
i. to prevent injury by increasing your ability to recover and by increasing flexibility.
ii. to build up endurance so that you can stay at your best, without flagging, for the whole game;
iii. to increase sharpness (speed, acceleration, decision making.)

Q2. Do I need to bother about pre-season preparation?

A. Yes. All serious cricketers will try to include pre-season preparation. For some, this may involve a fitness programme; for others it may be a matter of trying to work on one aspect of the game which needs special attention. If you are fortunate enough to attend a pre-season course [see page 70 for useful addresses] or you live within range of indoor coaching facilities, then you start with a clear advantage. However, for most players, the school or club season will not begin until late April or the beginning of May so, while you are waiting to get started, try the PRE-SEASON TESTS at the end of this chapter…

Q3. A great deal is made of mental preparation. How important is this and how can I improve?

A. The key factor is that you realise this could be important. It is! Mental preparation takes the stress out of the moment, allowing you to concentrate,

Brian Lara (West Indies).

ready for what's ahead. You want to be relaxed but ready for action. Essentially, if you have decided that you want to play well - then prepare for it. Give yourself time, alone, to get your mind in order. Get your mental approach right and you will be well on the way towards success. Think about your role as an individual, and then as an important part of the team. Teach yourself to focus before and during a match. Keep your mind alert to what may be required at any given moment, and above all be positive - not negative. Be aware that you are strong enough to cope with any situation. Prepare yourself to achieve, not to fail.

Michael Atherton writes:

"Mental toughness is the key to success at the highest level. Toughness comes from within; it is a deep unshakable belief in your own ability - even when you are going through a difficult patch. It is a desire to fight for your team when times are hard and you are staring down the barrel. It is a knowledge of when the opportunity presents itself and of ramming home the advantage when the opposition is weakening. It is the ability to stick to your guns when all around you urge otherwise…"

Q4. It is common knowledge that certain players have loads of natural ability while others do not. Can those with less ever catch up?

A. Life is never completely fair! Clearly, at the beginning, it helps to be one of the talented ones. But equally important is to recognise how many of the "naturals" get bored with their ability and lose interest in the game - especially when the others begin to catch up. I believe that most sports people are looking for a challenge and there is a great deal an ambitious young player can do to help him/herself catch up or get ahead. So much depends on your mental attitude. If you want it enough - you'll probably get there. If you are serious about raising your game, then read on…

Q5. Should I have my own individual fitness programme?

A. It helps. Every individual is bound to need a different approach, to some extent. What works for others may not be right for you. If you can, get some expert assistance when planning your programme - but the following section may help…

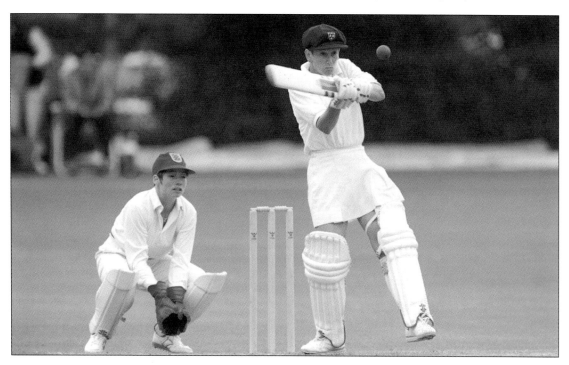

Women's cricket is fast-growing in popularity. All comments in this book apply to either the boys' or the girls' game.

B. MY ESSENTIAL FITNESS NEEDS

Many young players will be forced to train away from the facilities of club or school. Whatever your sport, you won't go far wrong if you can include three types of training in your general pattern: FLEXIBILITY, SPEED, ENDURANCE.

Where possible, always train with at least one partner.

1. FLEXIBILITY

Always start here…

Whatever your sport, you are recommended to include flexibility exercises or stretching exercises every day - even on non-training days.

It makes good sense to begin every session with gentle stretching in order to bring the muscles into use gradually. The "stretch" should never be savage - "mild discomfort" being the absolute limit. It must be a gradual stretch - not a jerk. Hold each position for a few seconds. After a hard match or work out it is an aid to relaxation if you can spend a few minutes working through your flexibility exercises. (The warm-down…)

2. SPEED TRAINING

To improve your SPRINTER SPEED - your speed in taking a quick single plus your ability to turn and sprint again - I use THE SHUTTLE TEST - see page 12

Allan Donald, South Africa's record breaking pace bowler. He puts much of his success and fitness down to regular flexibility exercises.

3. ENDURANCE

This is where you build up your ability to keep going for long periods without losing your skill level. Endurance is improved by proper training over months not weeks. It fits well into the off-season period.

Steady running of 1 to 3 miles - several times a week. Run in pleasant surroundings if you can - on the beach or in the hills - but do it! You are building up basic endurance which will be vital later in the season…

But, be aware:

It is quite usual to improve steadily when training sessions begin, but be prepared to reach the first rest phase or no progress stage. This is a period when many uninformed young athletes lose heart and believe they will never improve any further. Stick at it for several weeks and gradually you will work your way into the next progress zone. Be aware that fitness, like learning, tends to improve in steps - followed by rest periods.

Top line bowlers must be fit.

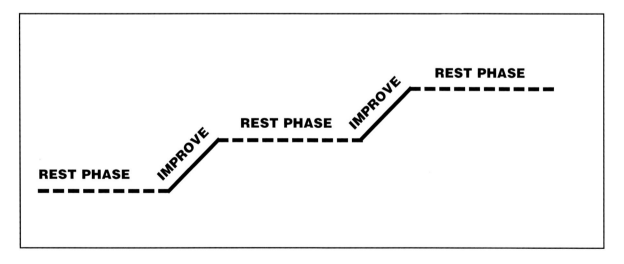

You only have to watch the world's best fielding sides to realise what an advantage they have. If you mean to play to a competitive level - you need to be in the best condition possible. This means not only must you be physically fit - you must be mentally strong - fitter and stronger than your opponents.

Quite simply, unless you believe this, and mean to act to improve both areas of fitness, you might just as well take up another sport - or settle for second best…

11

C. TEST YOURSELF

What sort of scores should I get?
Take these tests and record your own set of results.
Your first target is to improve on your own performance.
There is a core of fitness and all-round skills which every young cricketer should aim to improve. Off season development may make a great difference when the new season starts again...

1. CATCHING REACTION TEST

Sharpen your SPEED and REACTIONS.

Tennis ball co-ordination test.
Use a tennis ball and a blank wall.
Mark a chalk line, say, 15 feet from the wall.
How many times can you throw and catch in 30 seconds?
Add several reaction tests of your own. Record your score and improve next time.
Give yourself a good work out of catching and fielding reaction work. Better still, work with a partner and test each other.

2. FOOTBALL AGILITY SKILL

Improve your footwork and agility.

All footballers work on this. It's excellent for footwork and it's satisfying to watch the improvement.
How many times can you keep the ball off the ground?
You may include headers as well as foot or knee bounces.
Keep your score. Any number over 50 shows a good level of skill.
Again, if you can work with a partner to build up a combined score, it makes an even better agility test.

3. THE SHUTTLE TEST

The RUN FOUR or quick singles speed test.

With or without a bat.
Mark out two points, 5 or 10 metres apart.
The closer the points, the more of an agility test it becomes. Later, you can stretch it out to represent a full match wicket...

See how many times you can "shuttle" back and forth between the two points in, say, 30 seconds. Record your score. Rest for one minute and then repeat.
See if you can maintain "good form" for 5 runs. Ideally, your partner will take turns with you. Time each other; compete with each other. Try to keep the rest periods to the same, precise time.
As you get fitter, you can increase the Shuttle Sprint time or distance.

We want electric pace over 10 metres.

4. TENNIS BALL THROWING

Accuracy test.

Mark out a target on a blank wall and, from a set distance, say 10 paces, see how many times you can hit the target in 10 throws. Repeat from 20 paces. Record your results and watch the improvement.

5. PULLS UPS or PRESS UPS

Shoulder strength.

Decide for yourself what, precisely, you mean by a proper press up or pull up.
Press ups require a full dip to the ground; pull ups require the chin to touch the pull up bar with no assistance from a body swing or a kicking action.
Both exercises will give you a shoulder strength score to improve upon.

6. TRUNK CURLS

Abdominal or stomach strength

There are numerous ways of measuring abdominal strength. A simple test is all you need. Lie on a mat. Using stomach muscles (not arm movement) sit up far enough to touch knee-caps. Lie back again - until head touches the mat. Repeat sit ups as many times as possible in 30 seconds.

7. ENDURANCE RUN

3 or 4 laps of the field - or a longer run. Test yourself against the clock…

PERSONAL SCORECARD

NAME:

	1		2		3	
	Score	Date	Score	Date	Score	Date
1. SPEED CATCHING (30 SECS)						
2. FOOTBALL SKILL						
3. RUN FOUR SHUTTLE (30 SECS)						
4. THROWING ACCURACY (20 THROWS)						
5. PULL UPS						
6. TRUNK CURLS (30 SECS)						
7. ENDURANCE RUN						

Above: Coaching at Lilleshall.

Right: Darren Gough - England's opening bowler - took his 100th Test Wicket at Headingly in 1998. 6 for 42 v. South Africa and a hat-trick v. Australia at Sydney in 1999.

BOWLING TO WIN

> Including check points: • i. Basics • ii. Seam and Swing • iii. Spin

66 *The best advice I can offer an ambitious young bowler is to get out and work at it. It takes a deal of hard graft and determination but when the wickets start to tumble it's worth all the effort. You've got to be fit and, to a certain extent, you've got to be lucky. There will be plenty of times when you begin to think you are getting nowhere - and then the luck swings your way again. Bowling to win is what I do best but I enjoy batting and fielding almost as much. It helps enormously if you enjoy the big occasion and, believe me, when you find yourself fired up and bowling for England, with a Headingly crowd behind you, that takes a bit of beating!* **99**

DARREN GOUGH
Yorkshire and England

The photographs and diagrams in Bowling to Win show right armers in action. Be clear though that, right or left-handed, you will develop your own unique style of bowling. In this book we offer you standard methods which work for some bowlers but we stress yet again that it will be your own self-belief which really counts in the long run. There are no short cuts.

If you mean to become a front-line bowler you have to turn yourself into a skilful, deadly accurate bowler with the experience and confidence to take wickets. By all means, listen to the experts, study everything which is written in this chapter and then get out and practise until you make it happen.

Check points for the serious bowler...

Think about these comments - all from top-line bowlers.

i. *"My run-up is too long. It is causing lack of balance and rhythm at the crease."* (Pace bowler.)

ii. *"Use of the front arm is important to spinners and pace bowlers alike."*

iii. *"When I'm bowling well, I give the ball plenty of air."* (Spin bowler.)

iv. *"I need to pick up the front knee to achieve lean-back at the crease."*

v. *"A high bowling arm helps with bounce."*

vi. *"Positioning of the front foot is crucial."*

vii. *"All through my action, I keep my eyes on a spot..."*

viii. *"Spin bowling is an art which only a very few master."*

ix. *"On slower pitches, medium pacers are very often more effective than the quicker bowlers."*

x. *"At all times, a genuinely quick bowler can surprise even the best batsman."*

All young players will wish to experiment with different bowling actions.

Seek advice from an experienced coach when deciding which bowling style to develop. There is no short cut to success; it takes a life-time of learning and hours of careful practice to be one of the best.

Study the experts and stick at it....

"Give the ball plenty of air."

BASIC BOWLING

i. BASIC BOWLING

Master the Basic delivery first. Then we'll look at other types...

If you can regularly knock over the stumps, you'll be worth your place on most teams...

10 points to improve your bowling.

(1) Grip: It is a finger grip - not a palm grip.
Hold the ball with your first two fingers on or across the seam, and your thumb on the seam underneath the ball.

(2) Run up: Avoid too long a run up.
You need to be balanced and well in control. 8 to 10 strides should be sufficient for most bowlers.
Mark out your run and practice from that spot. Don't keep changing.

(3) Understand your target area.
Make sure you can bowl the accurate, standard ball. Every time you turn to bowl, you should have a mental picture of the ball you are trying to bowl.

Basic Grip
Ball is held in fingers not palm. Seam vertical between slightly spread first and second finger. Thumb on seam underneath.

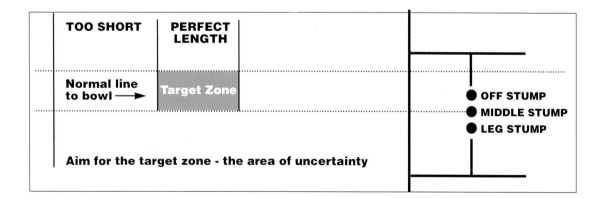

TOO SHORT	PERFECT LENGTH		
Normal line to bowl →	Target Zone		● OFF STUMP ● MIDDLE STUMP ● LEG STUMP
Aim for the target zone - the area of uncertainty			

Target the LINE of middle and off or the OFF STUMP. Become confident about hitting it regularly. The perfect, standard ball will take off the off-stump bail...

Target the LENGTH which has the batsman wondering whether to play forwards or back... Concentrate on Line and Length. Don't waste time with swing or pace until you can do this.

(4) "Head on" or "side on"?

This is important and needs the advice of an experienced coach.

HEAD ON

SIDE ON

Bowlers will have a natural style and after a year or two this will be difficult to alter. If you can, get an expert to watch you and iron out problems as soon as possible. Until recently, all bowlers were advised to get side on and, unless there is a sound reason, this action has more advantages than the head on style.

(5) Know the LBW laws.

The young bowler who appeals for every strike on the batsman's pads merely emphasises his lack of cricketing knowledge. See THE LAWS on page 66.

Learn these few key points...

a. If the ball pitches *outside the leg stump* - the batsman *cannot be out lbw.*

b. If the ball pitches *outside the off stump* and is padded away by the batsman, *he can still be out lbw* if the ball would have come back and hit the stumps (off spinner or in swing).

c. Don't appeal for lbw unless you are in a reasonable position to see. The bowler and keeper are the best placed.

Use the non-bowling arm as well.

18

Eyes on target. Side on position

BASIC BOWLING ACTION

Good attacking run up. Balance and rhythm.

(6) Know the NO BALL laws?

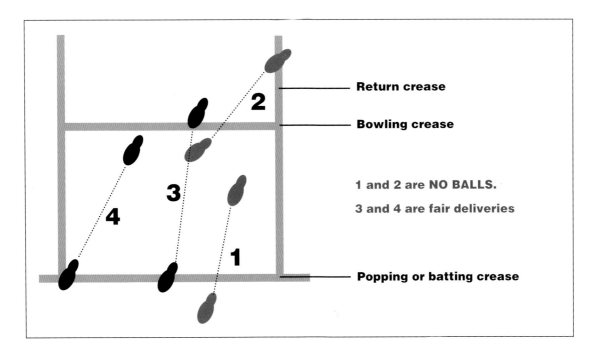

Return crease

Bowling crease

1 and 2 are **NO BALLS.**

3 and 4 are fair deliveries

Popping or batting crease

Good balance and delivery. Don't strain for extra pace.

Jason Gillespie. Australian pace bowler showing follow through.

(7) Bowl from close to the stumps.

Variety can be helpful but, unless you have a good reason for trying something else (see page 25), you should get in fairly close to the stumps and bowl "wicket to wicket". An umpire is far more likely to give you an lbw decision if he knows you are a "close in" bowler.

(8) Bowl "over the wicket".

(ie. with your bowling arm close to the line of the stumps.)

It may be sensible to come around the wicket to left-handers or to right-handers who have become used to your usual style…

Always try to keep the batsman guessing…

(9) The follow-through.

A good follow-through is a sign of balance and rhythm. You must, of course, avoid running on down the batting area - but the secret is to stay on line for as long as you can before moving off to the side.

(10) Find your own style.

The over-riding essential is to be able to bowl straight.

Whilst it is a fact that most top-line bowlers have their own individual techniques, young bowlers will do well to develop a bowling style which follows most of the above principles…

Above all – Don't strain for extra pace.

Dion Nash of NZ bowls for Middlesex v. Hampshire. Note the use of the left hand.

II. SEAM AND SWING BOWLING

"Attacking bowling can also be through being accurate and patient.

Frustrate the batsman by bowling at or just outside the off stump and "dry up the runs". The consistent bowler who can keep on putting the ball on the spot, ball after ball, is far more valuable than the out and out pace man who sprays the ball all over the place."

a. AWAY SWINGER (out swing)

Moves in the air from leg to off.
i. Point the seam towards third man.
ii. The rough side faces the off side
iii. At release, the little finger should be closest to the batsman.

iv. The ball is released off the index finger.
v. Bowling arm high.
vi. Bowl from close to the stumps.
vii. Pitch the ball well up to give it time to swing.
viii. Body side on for as long as possible.
ix. Front foot placed slightly across the crease towards the leg side.
x. Arm follows through across the body.

GRIP FOR OUTSWING
Seam is angled slightly to off-side. First and second fingers slightly apart. Side of thumb on seam. shiny side of ball on leg-side.

Glenn McGrath. Australia's successful strike bowler.

b. IN SWINGER

Moves in the air from leg to off.

i.   Point the ball towards fine leg.
ii.   Rough side faces the leg side
iii. At release, the thumb should be closest to the batsman.
iv.   The ball should be released off the middle finger.
v.   Bowling arm very high.
vi.   More of a straight on body position.
vii. Front foot placed slightly to the off side.
viii. Arm follows through to the right leg.

GRIP FOR INSWING

Waquar Younnis (Pakistan) specialist pace bowler, famous for reverse swing.

c. OFF-CUTTERS and LEG-CUTTERS

The off-cutter is the main variation for the away swing bowler. Instead of moving away towards the slips, the ball is cut back or straightened by the use of the index finger.

The leg cutter goes the other way and is the alternative delivery for an in swing bowler. The ball is gripped as for the in swinger but then adjusted slightly until the middle finger lies on the seam. On delivery, the middle finger pulls across the seam in anti-clockwise direction, rather like a quick leg break....The aim is to cut back or straighten the ball.

LEG-CUTTER

OFF-CUTTER

SEAM BOWLING

The seam bowler aims to hit the pitch with the seam vertical. Use the standard basic grip. Seam and swing are for the medium pacer who relies on accuracy and variety rather than pace...

QUICK BOWLING

Really quick, natural bowlers are rare. Most young players will have a shot at "quick bowling" but will be advised to concentrate first on achieving a reasonable degree of accuracy.

At times, a genuinely quick bowler can surprise even the best of batsmen - and for this reason there is often a place for the "quickie".

III. SPIN BOWLING

"It's not like being a fast bowler who can take out his frustrations on a batsman if he's being hit. As a spinner, it's a longer process. You might get hit for four sixes in a row and then take a wicket with the next ball. That's fine."

"I never got picked in age-group sides. Either I wasn't good enough or I wasn't the right person. But I decided that I wanted to bowl leg-breaks so I soaked up as much information as I could about guys who bowled them…. Then I just practised and practised in the nets and after a while I got picked."

SHANE WARNE
Australia

Mustaq Ahmed (Pakistan) - close to stumps.

Anil Kumble (India) - wide of stumps.

LEG-SPIN (Wrist spin)

Turns from leg to off.

GRIP:

i.   Hold the ball across the seam.
ii. Extend the bowling arm straight towards the ground.
iii. Cock the wrist with the palm towards the face.
iv. Wedge the ball between the 1st, 2nd and 3rd fingers.

ACTION:

i.   Normal side on action.
ii. Bowling arm comes through slightly lower than vertical.
iii. Keep the palm facing the batsman.
iv. Rotate wrist powerfully from right to left at release. "Turn the door knob."

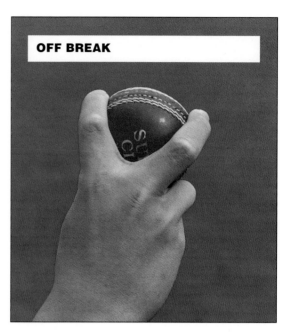

OFF BREAK

LEG BREAK

Top joint of first finger, gripping across seam, is main spinning 'lever'. Second finger, widely spaced, also grips across seam.

As the ball is bowled, the wrist is 'cocked' back and flicks forward with the first finger dragging sharply downwards and thumb flipping upwards.

After delivery, hand cuts across body and finishes with palm pointing upwards.

OFF-SPIN (Finger spin)

Spins from off to leg.

GRIP:

i.   Hold the ball across the seam.
ii. Wedge the ball between the 1st and 2nd fingers.

Third finger cups ball and lies along to impart the leg spin.

Wrist is bent inwards and only flips straight as ball is delivered.

Third and fourth fingers flick up-ward and for-wards, whilst thumb side of hand points down-wards.

ACTION:

i.   Closed action.
ii. Short front stride, pivoting hard on front foot.
iii. Rotate wrist powerfully from left to right. "Turn the door knob".
iv. Keep fingers on top of the ball.

WRONG 'UN (or GOOGLY)

Looks like a leg spinner but turns from off to leg...

This is the leg spinner's alternative ball. The leg spin action alters as little as possible but the wrist is twisted further so that the ball comes out of the back of the hand and on pitching behaves like an off break.

GRIP:

As for leg spin.

ACTION:

i.   Normal side on action.
ii. Bowling arm comes through slightly lower than vertical.
iii. Keep back of the hand facing the batsman.
iv. Rotate the wrist powerfully from left to right at release. "Turn the door knob behind you."

TOP SPIN

Drops sharply and bounces higher.

GRIP:

As for leg spin.

ACTION:

i.   Normal side on action.
ii. Bowling arm comes through slightly lower than vertical.
iii. Keep the back of the hand closest to your head.
iv. Rotate wrist powerfully at release. "Turn the door knob beside you."

FLOATER

An essential ball for the successful off spinner. Instead of exerting the usual spin, the ball is pushed towards the off stump.

LEFT-ARM BOWLING.

Because there are not so many left-handed bowlers, it can be a big advantage to pick one. By bowling over the wicket at middle and off the quick or medium paced left-hander introduces a change in the direction of attack.

Left arm spinners usually bowl round the wicket and move the ball away from the right-handed batsmen.

And remember...

Many top line bowlers do things differently!

If you have your own special way of bowling - and it works - then it may be sensible to stick to what you do well. Before you alter your style and become "correct" just check with an expert who can advise you.

IMPROVE YOUR BATTING

Including: • 1 Batting essentials • 2. Defence • 3. Attack

" *The most successful batsmen I know work really hard to improve their game. Much of their success is down to natural ability and the will to succeed but it is also crucial to have the help of an experienced adviser. In competitive cricket you must be willing to listen to advice, to develop your own technique and to take action to eliminate weaknesses. If you are not prepared to work at it, you won't go far in this game.*

How good you eventually become depends to a great extent on your own self belief and on your determination to keep improving. Batting does not always come easy and you have to be prepared to work your way through the difficult spells as well as the successful times. If you really mean to be a cricketer, you've got to want it! "

NASSER HUSSAIN
Essex and England

Opposite: Nasser Hussain - front-line England batsman. 207 v. Australia - Edgbaston 1997.

1. BATTING ESSENTIALS

Top batsmen will run through a basic list like this every season.

Take nothing for granted and make your own success...

I. KIT CHECK

Select a suitable bat.
Far too many young players are trying to play with bats which are too large or heavy and which restrict the range of strokes.
Ensure that pads, gloves, protector(s) and shoes/boots are comfortable.
You need your kit to permit freedom to run quick singles....

II. GRIP

Lay the bat flat on the ground. Pick up bat like an axe.
Hands together. Thumbs and fingers around the handle. V's in line.

Which hand controls the shot?
Grip controlled by top hand for vertical bat shots (Drive and Defence). Bottom hand contact with thumb and forefinger only.
Grip controlled by bottom hand for horizontal bat shots (Cut, Hook and Pull).

III. STANCE

Side on or open stance...?
Side on.
Ask for 'Middle Stump'. Seek advice before changing your guard.
Feet shoulder width apart. Knees slightly bent; eyes level.
weight evenly distributed to enable movement. Head above the feet.
Place bat in a position to allow a straight back lift.

Most coaching manuals favour the side on stance; usually, keeping one foot just inside the crease. However there are times when a batsman may prefer to use a more open stance - sometimes facing directly down the wicket. A number of Test players do this when, for example, facing a really good leg spinner.
    But think it through and in normal circumstances favour the side on stance.

And when might you take up a stance just outside your batting crease?

Clearly, it would make a difference if the wicket-keeper is standing up or back?

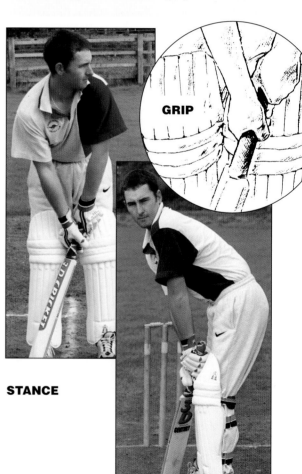

GRIP

STANCE

IV. BACKLIFT

When you 'pick up' your bat - is it (a) over the stumps or (b) towards the slips?

How high do you lift the bat? Does this vary from bowler to bowler?

The advice for young players is as follows:

Usually, take the bat back straight over the stumps.
Toe of the bat about level with hands. (This varies with the speed of the bowler...)
Pick the bat up as the bowler nears the crease.
Avoid a late, hurried lift.

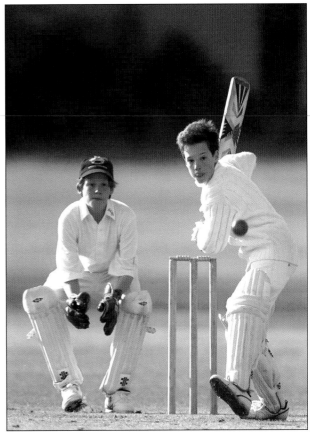

Many front-line Test batsmen may pick up over slip/gully area - but come down straight.

For example, if you are facing a really good leg spinner who is pitching the ball just outside the line of your leg stump - how do you intend to play him?

Try to work out the advantages or disadvantages of each style.

V. FOOTWORK

Good footwork is absolutely crucial for a batsman.

Power begins from the base - from getting your feet in the right position.

The Shuffle: the small movement of the feet to get the batsman into line and balance to play the ball correctly. Usually, a step back and across to cover the off stump. Get into position early.

VI. CONCENTRATION

How many times have you batted for more than an hour this season?

What method(s) do you use to help yourself to concentrate?

What prevents you from concentrating properly?

Concentration and fitness go together. If you can't concentrate - you won't make it as a cricketer. Study the top-line batsmen; watch how they keep their mind on the job in hand. Watch how they help the batsman at the other end by a quiet word between overs. Study for yourself the difference between the "top-line" batsman and the "bottom of the order" player.

VII. LEARN TO BUILD AN INNINGS

Before you go to the crease - have some quiet time on your own.

Prepare yourself mentally. Get your mind right. Get your eyes adjusted to the light.

When you get to the wicket - take your time. Show that you are in control.

In more competitive cricket, opponents will try to unsettle you. They may talk to distract you. They may alter the field placings - bringing in several close catchers and generally try to undermine your confidence.

Learn to build your innings… Target the first run; then 5; then 10; then 20….

Teach yourself to concentrate on the next ball - and nothing else…

Learn to take the rough with the smooth…You'll get the occasional "unplayable ball" - a Shane Warne special! You'll get the occasional "bad decision" or brilliant fielding and you'll get the odd "0" against your name. Learn from it and come back stronger than before. As a famous Yorkshire umpire was frequently heard to say: "It's no use moaning at me, lad. Look in t'scorebook. Tha'll see if tha was oot…"

VIII. RUNNING BETWEEN THE WICKETS

CALLING

i. Three clear calls. YES - NO or WAIT.

ii. Most calls are made by the striker.

iii. The non-striker calls when the striker is unsighted.

iv. When running more than a single, the batsman running to the danger end makes the final call.

BACKING UP

i. Non striker holds bat in the hand closest to the bowler.

ii. Move out of ground as the bowler releases.

iii. As the ball is about to be hit, the momentum continues but the size of the steps decreases to allow a change of direction and quick response to a call.

TURNING

i. Turn with the bat in the hand which allows best view of the ball if further runs may be available.

ii. When approaching the crease, decrease the running height of the last few strides.

iii. The bat should be pushed over the line from a low position that will allow the opposite hand to touch the ground.

[Use The Run 4 Shuttle p12 to improve speed and sharpness…]

RUNNING

i. Run the first run fast.

ii. If there may be more than one run, talk to your partner as you pass each other.

2. DEFENCE

Why "defence" before "attack"?

Your early aim must be to occupy the crease. Give yourself time to settle. Play yourself in... Offer no chance until you have found the feel of the wicket. You need to have your defence tight and to keep out the key ball which will beat you.

[Clearly, there will be situations - especially in limited overs games - when there is no time for the "build gradually" approach. Your captain has asked you to "go for quick runs" and you must throw caution to the wind on behalf of your team.]

Take time to master these two key defensive strokes.

I. FORWARD DEFENCE

Played to a good length ball in line with the wicket or just outside the off stump.

i. Step forward and across to the line of the ball.
ii. Front foot as near to the pitch of the ball as possible; just inside the line of the ball.
iii. Front knee bend allows body weight to get right forward, over the ball. Bat angled. No gap between bat and pad.
iv. The stroke is played with soft hands, without the intention of a forcing stroke.

Which of the following comments on DEFENCE is correct?

They all come from first class batsmen.

i.) "Foot well down the wicket. Get your nose over the ball..."
ii.) "Don't push the bat out in front of the pads..."
iii.) "Bend the front knee..."
iv.) "The closer you can get to the pitch of the ball, the easier it is to kill..."
v.) "Play it late - so that your eyes are directly over the ball..."
vi.) "Try to lead into the stroke with your head and your front shoulder."

DEMONSTRATE

PRACTICE

II. BACK DEFENCE

Played to a short-pitched ball on or just outside the off stump.

i.   Back foot moves well back and across the stumps to the line of the ball.

ii. Back foot points to Point. Front foot slides back until resting next to it - as per Batting Stance.

iii. The front elbow is high.

iv. The bat face is straight and angled forward to keep the ball down.

v.   The ball hits the bat; it is not a forcing stroke.

"Keep out the good ball. Hit the bad ball."

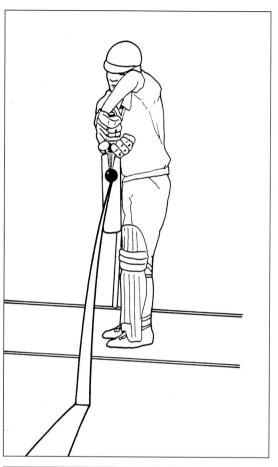

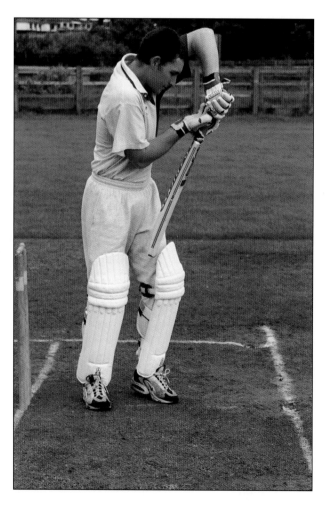

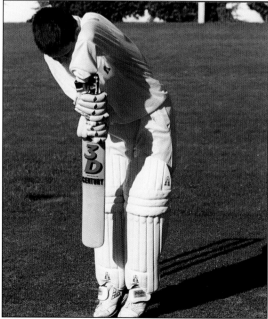

B. ATTACKING STROKES

Attacking batsmen aim to take control - to wrest the initiative away from the bowlers. But controlled attack requires patience and judgement. Force yourself to wait for the wayward ball.

Keep your cool at all times... Most bowlers will be hoping that you try a rash stroke off a good ball. Don't throw away your wicket...

Every batsman should master several attacking strokes. Don't try to cover them all at once; build up your repertoire - your own selection - and check that each one is good.

Alec Stewart, England's attacking captain, in action.

1. FRONT FOOT DRIVE

Played to a ball close to a half volley.
The stroke is almost identical to the FORWARD DEFENSIVE only in this case the ball is struck...

i.   Step forward and across to the line of the ball - onto heel and then toe. This will carry the head to the line of the ball.

ii. Rock back with the back lift and then forward with contact made level with the front leg.

iii. The bat is moving when contacting the ball. The quicker the bat moves, the more powerful the drive.

Right: Sir Garfield Sobers.

2. BACKFOOT DRIVE

Played to a ball short of a length that will reach the batsman above waist height.

As for the BACKWARD DEFENSIVE only this time the ball is forced away for runs.

3. THE PULL STROKE

Steve Waugh (Australia).

Generally played to a short delivery, missing the stumps on the leg side.

i.   Back foot moves back and outside the line of the ball;

ii. Swivel on back foot to open up the body

iii. High bat lift allows downward strike to keep the ball on the ground.

iv. Body weight moves from back foot onto front foot…

v.   Contact ball with arms extended in front of body.

vi. Aim to hit the ball in front of square leg.

4. THE HOOK

Played to a very short pitched, lifting ball which if left will pass over the batsman's shoulder.

Not the same as the pull, the hook is played to a higher ball. This shot should only be played by competent batsmen and in most cases it is good sense to avoid playing at the ball at all. However, if you do try it, the mechanics are much as for the lower, pull stroke.

i.   Step back and across towards the off stump.
ii. Ensure that the head is inside the line of the ball.
iii. Bat starts high; aim to hit down on the ball behind square leg.
     Balance is crucial.
     Keep eyes on the ball.

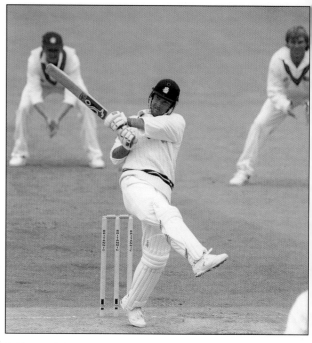

G. Thorpe of Surrey (vs Northants.)

5. THE SQUARE CUT

Graham Thorpe. England v. West Indies at Lords. Outstanding left hand batsman with a Test average of over 40.

Played to a widish, short delivery outside the off stump.

Step back.
High backlift.
Hit down on the ball.
Bent back knee gives good balance.
Strike ball with arms extended.
Don't try the cut if the ball is too close to your body.

6. LEG GLANCE

Short of a length, on leg stump.

Similar to the backward defensive shot.
Allow the ball to come on and direct it behind square leg.
It is a glance - not a strike.
Let the pace of the ball do most of the work...

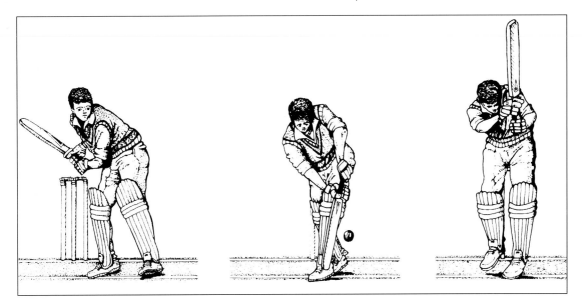

7. THE SWEEP

Played to a good length ball pitching outside the leg stump. Hit the ball down.

(The reverse sweep is seen in Limited Overs games but is not recommended for junior players, except under exceptional circumstances...)

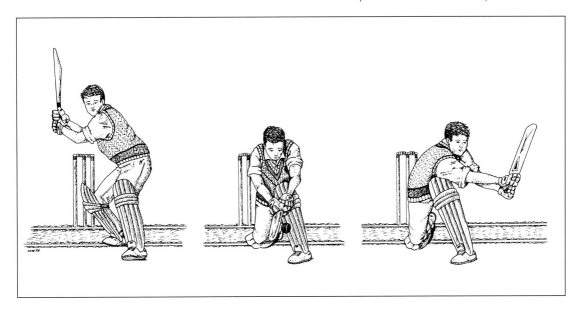

39

The LEFT HANDER

There are certain definite advantages in being a left-handed batsman.

Bowlers see many more right-handers and have to alter their angle of attack. Many bowlers will switch to bowl 'around the wicket' but, again, this often causes them to make slight alterations in their run-up and rhythm. Another important advantage is that to have a left hander at the wicket with a right-hander will cause frequent changes and a degree of uncertainty for bowlers and for fielders. Of course, a real problem arises when a left-hander has to face a really good leg-spinner on a turning wicket who can put the ball into the foot-marks of the earlier bowlers.

LOOKING AFTER YOUR CRICKET BAT

A little bit of understanding may allow a good bat to last many years.

i. With a new bat.
    A light oiling - especially around the toe area. Oil the blade, toe and sides but avoid the back and shoulders.
    Take plenty of time to knock it in properly. A minimum of 3 to 4 hours is helpful.

ii. After an innings…
    A slight sanding to clean off the surface.
    A few taps from a bat mallet to tidy up any bruised areas.
    Don't over-oil. The bat becomes heavy and dead.
    Use a dry cloth to clean off after a game. Don't wash the bat with water.

iii. And remember:
    The bat surface will get marked - especially if long innings are played.
    Don't use your bat against poor quality or hard cricket balls.

Matthew Elliot. Attacking opening bat for Australia.

Two ways of avoiding the bouncer. Eyes on the ball for as long as possible.

DUCK　　　　**SWAY**

COMPETITIVE FIELDING AND CATCHING

> Including: • Field positions chart • i. Improve your ground fielding • ii. Safer catching

66 *Outstanding fielders inspire any team. It takes discipline and determined concentration to reach the highest standards but it should be a key focus area for every ambitious side. Just as a top-line keeper is crucial, so a really competitive fielding team can gain a huge advantage… The best players include regular, sharp practice sessions - where possible under match conditions. They know that in today's competitive game, fielding and catching must be of the highest possible standard.* **99**

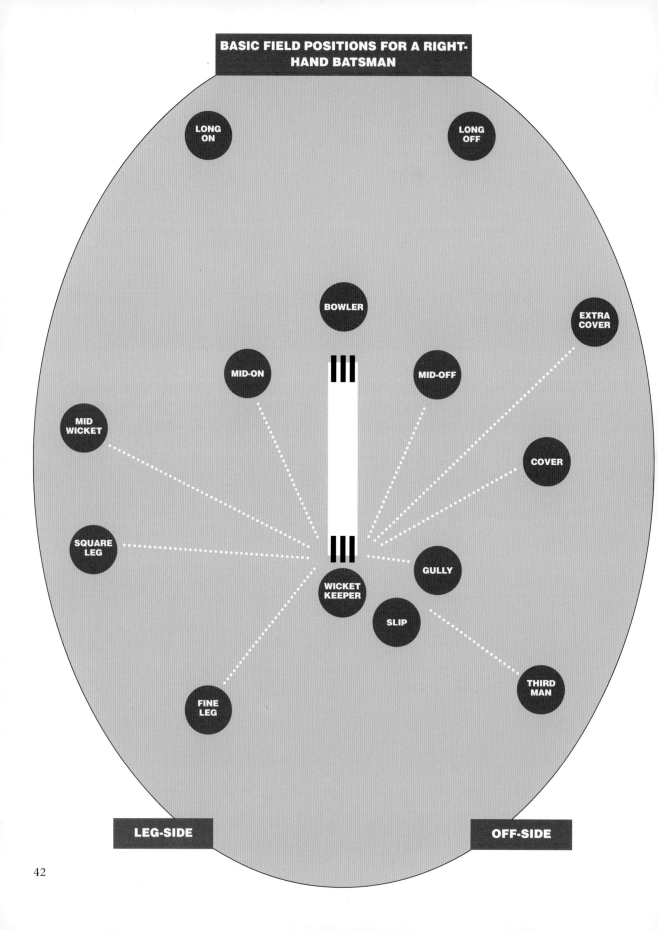

BASIC FIELD POSITIONS FOR A RIGHT-HAND BATSMAN

LONG ON

LONG OFF

BOWLER

EXTRA COVER

MID-ON

MID-OFF

MID WICKET

COVER

SQUARE LEG

GULLY

WICKET KEEPER

SLIP

THIRD MAN

FINE LEG

LEG-SIDE

OFF-SIDE

1. WHEN THE BALL IS ON THE GROUND

It is important to be clear about your aim with each type of fielding exercise.

1. THE LONG BARRIER SAFETY STOP

Used when out in the deep field.

Prevent the boundary at all costs. Ensure that the barrier is "watertight" and practise this until you are really confident.

Often, it is necessary for a "safety" fielder to remain right on the boundary edge giving as much time as possible to try to prevent the boundary ball. In such a case, the fielder will not walk in with the bowler…

II. ATTACKING THE BALL

The batsmen are considering taking a quick run.

i. Be "on the move" as the ball is played,
ii. Attack the ball - arrive in balance - eyes on the ball NOT wickets.
iii. Be prepared to use a quick under-hand flick (see below) to get the ball in faster than a full throw.

Once the batsmen realise that an aggressive fielding side means business they may well become nervous about attempting risky singles. Top fielders spend ages 'attacking' the ball, picking up cleanly and throwing down the stumps. Cover point is often the specialist fielder - but most other positions can be improved by a fielder with an attacking attitude. Beware of the over-anxious player who creeps in too close and is easily passed by a skilful stroke-maker. It requires experience in match conditions to judge just when to move and how quickly to come in.

III. RETRIEVING

The sliding stop - which throws the body feet first ahead of the speeding ball - is an athletic and effective method for expert cricketers and has raised the standard of attacking fielding to a new level.

IV. UNDERARM RUN-OUT

Used in close when there is a chance of a run-out and no time for a pick up and throw.

Often it involves a quick swoop and an under-arm flip to the keeper. Sometimes is needs a full-length underarm dive-pass, not unlike a rugby scrum-half. Frequently it is so close that only a direct hit on the stumps will gain the run out.

It is an important skill which needs regular practice under match conditions.

2. CATCHING

How many times have you been told that "catches win matches"?

Every player can improve his catching by following the correct technique and by regular practice, but different fielding positions bring different types of catching.

Essentially, you need to practise all the catches listed below.

If you are not confident about your catching ability, I suggest you try to specialise in one particular fielding position for a while. This way you may be able to get used to a certain type of catch coming your way. But beware, whenever a captain tries to "hide" a weak catcher, he can be sure that the next chance will come to precisely this man! The only solution lies in regular match practice.

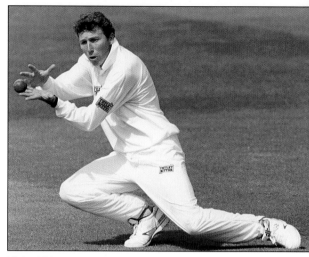
Michael Atherton - brilliant close catcher.

1. SLIP OR CLOSE CATCHING

Stay low to the ground
Hands together - do not point the fingers at the ball.
Watch the ball - at 1st or 2nd Slip.
Watch the edge of the bat - everywhere else.

Concentration is the key. If you have the reactions and ability to field close, it can be a real test. Some players will have the hands in front of the body in catching position; others will leave the hands on the knees in resting position until the last moment. Whilst I favour the first, there have been some remarkable slip fielders who are happy with the latter. What really matters is that you are alert and low. You must be low enough to guarantee that nothing can get beneath you; it's easier to drive 'up' for a catch than to get 'down'. [Ask any goal keeper…]

As the ball is touched by the batsman, you must be onto your toes…

II. OUTFIELD CATCHING THE HIGH CATCH

Run quickly to get under the ball.
Eyes on the ball.
Be still for the catch.
Catch the ball with the hands extended above the eyes.
Withdraw hands towards the shoulder as the ball makes contact.
Cradle the ball.

Judgement is the key here. With the high ball, the secret is to move quickly into place and to be still as you take the catch. But how often can the catcher arrange to have the perfect ball. Frequently, you are on the move, in a swirling wind and sometimes with another fielder rushing towards you as anxious as you are to attempt the catch. A loud cry of "my ball" is essential - but after that it's up to your judgement. One extra bit of coaching advice I offer is that, as with a high rugby ball, you should aim to take the ball with the whole body. Cradle the ball.

Allow your legs and body to give with the ball.

Jack Russell is one of the best known and most successful wicket-keepers in world cricket.

THE ART OF WICKET-KEEPING

8 key points for the young keeper

> **66** *If you want to keep wicket in a top-class side you must be prepared to study the art. Easily the best advice I can offer a young keeper is to go and watch a specialist in action. Try to get to a real match, with a competitive edge, and spend a session studying the man with the gloves.*

At any level, the wicket-keeper's performance is an instant guide to the quality of a fielding side. The keeper is always involved, always at the centre of the game and of considerable importance to the success and confidence of each individual bowler. Runs saved behind the stumps can be crucial. A keeper's attitude and alertness can greatly influence those about him; if the keeper enjoys his game it usually shows in his actions. If he can also make good runs, batting at number 6 or 7 in the order, he becomes even more valuable to his team.

See how you get on with the points which follow.... **99**

JACK RUSSELL

Gloucestershire and England.

KEY POINTS FOR THE YOUNG KEEPER

1. STANCE

Be comfortable and well balanced.

Don't add pressure by getting into the stance position too early.

i.   Feet shoulder width apart
ii. Crouch on the balls of the feet
iii. Hands on the ground.

2. GENERAL TAKE

Assume that every ball will reach you. Ride and give with the ball.

i.   Hands together.
ii. Point fingers up or down - never at the line of the ball.
iii. Reach out for the ball and receive the ball with soft hands.
iv. In run out situations, always receive the ball behind the stumps.
v.   When there is no run out possibility, attempt to catch all throwing returns on the full.

3. STANDING BACK - TO PACE

Adopt a position similar to that of a goal-keeper when facing a penalty.

i. Stand at the point where you can comfortably receive the ball as it begins its descent.
ii. On both leg and off side, try to receive the ball with the body outside the line of the ball. This allows you to be in balance when you take the ball. The feet must move.

4. STANDING UP AND STUMPING - TO SPIN

i.   Stand right up to the stumps - within stumping range.
ii. Stay down until the ball has bounced. Move to the ball as late as you can.
iii. Only move your hands in a stumping manner when a stumping is possible, ie. fully receive the ball.

TAKING THE WIDER BALL
(OFF-SIDE)

TAKING THE WIDER BALL
(LEG-SIDE)

Body poised forward and towards wicket.

Body moves off the line of the ball just before the "take" giving free arm movement towards wicket.

Palms face ball. Head stays down. Do not move too quickly from stance position - wait - and move quickly after picking up line and length.

5. TAKING ON THE LEG SIDE

This is more difficult and requires careful foot work to keep within strike range of the stumps. If you go too early, you'll find that you will lose sight of the ball too soon, because the batsman obscures your line of vision. Work your feet across parallel to the stumps.

6. FITNESS AND PRESSURE COACHING

Like every conscientious cricketer, a wicket-keeper must be fit for his job. Keeping wicket involves quick reactions, and a sound technique which only comes from careful study of the requirements. It also requires an extra dose of concentration. If you enjoy the challenge of being at the centre of the action and are willing to take a few blows - then wicket-keeping may be for you. The exercises listed on page 12 will help but there is no substitute for putting on the gloves and having a concentrated pressure work-out with a helpful coach.

7. SPECIALIST EQUIPMENT

Gloves should be comfortable and close fitting. Rather than have an over-sized pair, use inners. If possible, buy your own gloves and don't be influenced into lending them to other part-time keepers. Wear a cap for protection and make sure that protector and pads are comfortable.

8. CONCENTRATION

Concentration is the key to successful catching. Your attitude should be determined and aggressive - "I'm going to get that ball, wherever it goes" but you have to learn to combine this aggression with relaxation. Aim for soft hands rather than a hard wall. Ride and give with the ball.

REMINDERS...

1. Up or back - never in no man's land.

2. Eye on the ball - not the bat.

3. Stay down - especially when standing up to the wicket.

4. Don't snatch. Ride and give with the ball.

5. Use gloves not pads...

6. Concentrate.

TEAM PLAYER?

> *Competitive cricket is a demanding team game. The most successful teams learn to bring the best out of each other - especially under severe pressure.*
>
> *Everyone interested in the game knows that there is far more to a good cricket X1 than just one individual's performance. Captains need team players - both on and off the field - who can learn to fit their personal skills and ambitions into the team's effort.*
>
> *As a senior umpire, I see many of the top teams working at close quarters. Success seems to breed success and it is noticeable that most of the best sides show the value of strong team-work - led by strong-minded captains and backed by hard-working committees and efficient back-room teams whose pride in the team's performance matches that of the players. I cannot over-emphasise the need for young cricketers - and those who guide them - to begin to understand how much the entire game can be improved by a deeper grasp of what is meant by team-work.*
>
> *Learn the special art of bringing the best out of your colleagues and you will be worth a place on most teams.*

DAVID SHEPHERD

*Former Gloucestershire player.
Test Match umpire since 1985.*

51

I. YOUR PLACE IN THE TEAM

Cricket is a demanding team game. Every player knows that there is far more to a good cricket X1 than just one outstanding individual's performance; the real game is about learning to combine the strengths of your entire team. Every individual must learn to think beyond his own selfish ambitions. The more you can blend your personal ambitions into the team's effort, the more you will be valued as a team player…It takes experience and great skill to build a team which can stay strong under pressure - but this must be the target for all thinking cricketers.

A very simple reminder… but one for all team players… involves: "THE 5 C's".

CONFIDENCE.

The best teams have the confidence and self belief to enjoy tough, competitive cricket. Without confidence no player can perform at his best

CO-OPERATE.

The key to team-work is unselfish support for colleagues, coaches and captain. How much the stronger characters help the weaker players will probably determine your success as a team.

COMPETE.

Every individual in your team must be fiercely determined competitors and very difficult to demoralise.

CONTROL.

Especially when the tension is on and emotions run high - your players keep control under pressure.

CHARACTER.

Your team will judged by its results - but also by its high standards and generous sportsmanship.

You play for the enjoyment of both teams and, win or lose, you can smile and shake hands with opponents afterwards.

Nor is the team found only on the match square…

Behind every successful player and every top team there will be many vital members who are seldom seen on the field of play. Success involves an efficient background team working together to produce the quality on match days. Stop for a moment to spare a thought for those who make your game possible: fixture organisers, ground staff, tea ladies, drivers.

A thoughtful team player will take time out to put in a word of thanks for some of what goes on behind the scenes. You can play a hugely important part for your club by supporting and appreciating the background team….

II. TEAM AIMS

If you say that you play to win - you over-simplify the game. There is much more to it…

Individual players must enjoy their cricket.
Of course - but what do we mean by "team enjoyment"?

The successful team manages to work together to satisfy all its members; not only to challenge every individual but to combine achievement and pleasure. The ideal team is made up of players who are not only good performers but who are genuinely interested in other people's enjoyment as well as their own. Undoubtedly, it helps to win but there has to be much, much more to the game than that…

We don't enjoy the company of selfish players who care little for their colleagues or, indeed, for the opposition. We do value sympathetic players - players who will support one another, fielders who encourage bowlers, strong batsmen who help the weaker players, uncomplaining players who back their captain; captains who…. etc. etc.

Most of us will recognise that we are good enough team players when we are winning - the test comes when things begin to go wrong… If we are one of the whingers (the moaners), if we are always looking for someone else to blame, if we are the type of player who hangs his head under pressure - we are no team player.

Or perhaps you are the positive competitor who has the strength of character to rally your team when the pressure gets stronger?

The single most important point to register is that you, as an individual, have an important part to contribute as a team player.

III. CAPTAINCY

Respect cannot be demanded - it has to be earned.

The right captain will have a major influence on his team.

When choosing a young captain, I look for certain key qualities:

I want a competitive captain who:

i. Has the respect of his team-mates;
ii. Will listen to his coach's advice and try to act upon it.

Nearly always he will be a better than average player, with a good knowledge of the game. Frequently he will be very competitive but one who has learned to control his aggression and his own ambitions. Ideally he will have a gift for encouraging the best from those around him and he must be prepared to learn. So long as he will listen to his coach, and so long as the two of them can work together, then there is plenty to build on. An arrogant captain (or a coach) who thinks he knows all the answers can be a disaster!

It would take a complete book to discuss the special role of the captain in any detail but I list 5 sound basics which should help any young player who is invited to take the job:

i. Lead by example on and off the field. Set the standards for your team and be prepared to talk to individual players about what you require.
ii. Be positive and cheerful.
iii. Believe in discipline but try not to criticise your players in public.
iv. Know your players well enough to get the best out of them.
v. Work with and offer support to your team coach and any match officials.
See page 62 for TACTICS QUIZ.

IV. THE COACH

Coaches, too, have their different styles. Just as a captain needs "player respect" so of course does a coach. A "team" player will understand this and lend support.

Sensitive coaches will be well aware of the atmosphere around them and will value players who genuinely try to help. Your "team contribution" could be to encourage a helpful player/coach atmosphere, to build a feel-good factor which allows both coach and players to make the very best use of the time available. A good coach will be trying to give you a positive session but what he may not tell you is how difficult it is to satisfy every one of his group at the same moment.

V. UMPIRES AND SCORERS

As with first-class referees in football or rugby, quality cricket umpires and scorers will help a game to flow. Theirs is an unselfish art which comes from years of dedication. Frequently they are former players themselves - players who enjoyed their sport and who wish to allow others to do the same. Nearly always, they know the game and its laws far better than the average player. In this book I do not attempt to tackle the complex art of the umpires and the scorers - I wish only to pay tribute to those who make the game possible for the rest of us.

VI. THE BACKGROUND TEAM

It is basic courtesy for every member of a team to thank the match officials after every game but take time out to spare a thought for those who make up the rest of the background teams: the fixture secretary, the groundsman, the changing room cleaner, the drivers, the person who provides you with clean kit or the match tea. Don't allow the season to pass without making sure that these people realise you are grateful - indeed, you should go out of your way to help in whatever way you can. Don't always leave it to the coach or the captain to say the thank yous. If you take pride in your school or your club team, ensure that visiting sides or supporters receive a friendly word of welcome. You lose nothing - and you gain a great deal.

Win or lose, you want your visitors to speak warmly about your club.

We have dealt only briefly with these matters but they deserve careful attention. If you are serious about your cricket you will realise that the authors are trying to make you stop and think more deeply about areas of the game which too many inexperienced players neglect…

VII. TOP TEAM CHECK LIST

One way to assess the quality of a club or a school team is to try the following TEST.

Think for a moment of the finest sports TEAM you know.

(Chose any sport. All Blacks - rugby; a cricket team, your favourite football team….)

How do they measure up to the following check list…?

Marks out of 10, in the column 1 boxes provided.

1. A CLUB TO BE PROUD OF? Does the club have plenty of senior players, officials and supporters who genuinely care about the standards of the club?

1) ☐ /10   2) ☐ /10

2. PLAYER ATMOSPHERE? Is there a good player spirit? Do the players encourage each other?

1) ☐ /10   2) ☐ /10

3. PLAYER / COACH ATMOSPHERE? Is there a good player/coach relationship? Are the players keen to keep learning and improving?

1) ☐ /10   2) ☐ /10

4. SKILL and FITNESS? Does the team possess the skill and the fitness to reach a high level?

1) ☐ /10   2) ☐ /10

5. DETERMINATION? Do the players practise hard? How do they react when things get difficult?

1) ☐ /10   2) ☐ /10

6. APPEARANCE? Do the players look smart/ business-like both on and off the pitch?

1) ☐ /10   2) ☐ /10

7. WELCOME FROM THE PLAYERS? Are visitors and/or new members made to feel welcome?

1) ☐ /10   2) ☐ /10

8. EXAMPLE? What sort of example do the players set? Do they show sportsmanship, courtesy and good manners - or are they arrogant and a poor example to those who look up to them? Do they care about the game?

1) ☐ /10   2) ☐ /10

9. BACKROOM TEAM? Does the club have a backroom team which takes care of many of the non-playing details (pitch quality / club house conditions / fixtures / treatment of visitors)?

1) ☐ /10   2) ☐ /10

10. COACHING? Is the coaching of a high standard? Is there a thriving junior section to the club, bringing on the next young players?

1) ☐ /10   2) ☐ /10

Now try the same test on your own team.
Marks out of 10 in the column 2 boxes…

Less than 5 out of 10 for any section leaves plenty of room for improvement.

TEST YOUR CRICKET KNOWLEDGE

QUIZ 1

NAME THE PLAYERS.

1/8:

All these pictured players are/were top-line International figures.
How many can you name?
Can you offer any further information about their outstanding careers?

(1)

(2)

(3)

(4)

(5)

(6)

(7)

(8)

QUIZ 2

SELECT YOUR TEAMS.

ENGLAND v. THE REST OF THE WORLD

You have been invited to select both teams. Which players would you select for a five-day Test Match to be played this summer - at Lords? You may select from today's players or players from yester-year.

In column 1: Select your strongest All Time England XI + 3 reserves.

In column 2: Select your All Time World XI + 3 reserves.

[Indicate: Batting order; *for captain; wk for wicket-keeper; B1, B2, B3, B4 for bowlers.]

Problem selection areas?

Do you select three seam/quick bowlers? One/two spinners? Six batsmen? Five batsmen + an all-rounder? Do you go for a specialist wicket-keeper or a wicket-keeper/batsman who may score runs as well? And what about your captains?

Now compare your teams with those selected by a knowledgeable friend or adult - or check your teams against my selections on page 63.

ENGLAND XI	WORLD XI
1	1.
2	2.
3	3.
4	4.
5	5.
6	6.
7	7.
8	8.
9	9.
10	10.
11	11.
Reserves:	Reserves:
1	1.
2	2.
3	3.

QUIZ 3

20 questions about BATTING.

1. What is meant by the following batting terms:
   (i) one short;
   (ii) backing up?

2. Explain
   (i) Long hop
   (ii) Half volley.

3. When a batsman "picks up" the bat in the bat-lift should it be:
   (i) towards the slips;
   (ii) over the middle stump;
   (iii) it may vary?

4. If the ball runs behind the wicket-keeper, which batsman should call for the first run?

5. What is the purpose of the shuffle (the small foot movement made before the ball arrives)?

6. Which hand should control the shots when the bat is vertical?

7. What advice would you give about "wrists" for the hook shot?

8. In defensive play, what is meant by "soft hands"?

9. If you hit the ball and it looks as if it may run onto your stumps - may you hit it again?

10. If after a mix-up over a run, both batsmen arrive at one end of the pitch - and the bails are removed at the other end - which batsman will be given run out?

11. If the ball is about to be caught and the batsman calls "mine!" what must be the umpire's decision?

12. How long must the fielders wait for the next batsman to appear?

13. If a batsman asks the umpire for a guard of "two", what does he mean?

14. If a batsman is not ready when the bowler starts his run-up, what should the batsman do?

15. A batsman who "carries his bat" achieves what?

16. Can a batsman appeal against
    (i) bad light
    (ii) fielders talking
    (iii) bowlers who run on the batting area
    (iv) the umpire's decision?

17. If a batsman is given out "caught behind" and knows that he did not hit the ball, may he appeal against the decision?

18. If a fielding captain decides that the umpire has mistakenly given out one of the opponents, may he call him back?

19. Explain what is meant by "building an innings".

20. If you had the chance to watch an innings by your 'favourite ever' batsman, who would you choose and why?

Answers on page 64.

QUIZ 4

20 questions about BOWLING.

1. Explain the no-ball rule for the front foot.

2. Can you show the grip for
   (i) standard
   (ii) in swing
   (iii) out swing bowling?

3. If the ball pitches outside the line of the leg stump, strikes the pad and would clearly have spun in to hit the wicket - is the batsman out?

4. What is the rule relating to a (non-striking) batsman who steps out of his crease before the bowler has let go of the ball? Can he be run out by the bowler?

5. What is the purpose of shining/polishing a new ball?

6. If the ball becomes wet, is it in order to ask the umpire for a cloth or towel to dry the ball before bowling?

7. Can a bowler change from "over the wicket" to "round the wicket" without informing the batsman?

8. An umpire warns a bowler for "running on the batting area". What happens if the bowler repeats the offence?

9. Is it in order for a bowler to ask an umpire to move back from the stumps?

10. What do you understand by the following terms:
    i). a beamer
    ii). a yorker

11. Why do coaches advise young bowlers to avoid over-long run-ups?

12. Can you show the correct grip for the off break and the leg break?

13. What is meant by a "green" pitch? Does this favour any type of bowler?

14. Why do most bowlers favour "over the wicket"?

15. What is a "googly"?

16. Should a bowler be "head on" or "side on"?

17. What is meant by "bowling to your field"?

18. How can a bowler "bowl defensively"?

19. How should the umpire signal a no ball?

20. Name your own all-time favourite bowler. Explain your choice.

Answers on page 64.

QUIZ 5

20 questions about

WICKET-KEEPING and FIELDING.

On the numbered diagram below, name the fielding positions:

1. _____

2. _____

3. _____

4. _____

5. _____

6. _____

7. _____

8. _____

9. _____

10. _____

(Check your answers against the diagram on page 42)

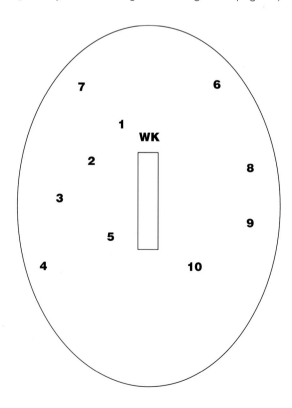

11. What advice is given for a "leg side take" by a keeper?

12. Explain what is meant by a fielder "backing up".

13. Is there any guide-line to help a wicket-keeper to decide whether to stand "up" or "back"?

14. When taking a high catch, give two pieces of advice for a fielder......

15. What advice on footwork could you offer a novice wicket-keeper?

16. What do you understand by a 5 to 4 field?

17. What type of bowler might need two slips and a gully?

18. When would you remove your slip fielder?

19. Why does a wicket-keeper often play with inners?

20. If a high ball appears a likely catch between two fielders, who should call, and what should he call?

Answers on page 64.

QUIZ 6

THE LAWS.

20 Questions.

1. If the ball hits a helmet or cap lying in the field of play, how many runs should be added to the batting total?

2. Which of these bowlers is bowling a "no ball"?
   (a) (b) (c) or (d)

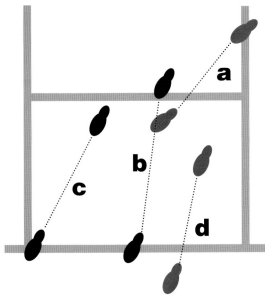

3. Can a batsman score any runs while the ball is in the air before he is caught out?

4. May the wicket-keeper take the ball in front of the stumps for a stumping?

5. If bowler mis-bowls and the ball comes to rest in front of the striker, what may the striker do?

6. If the square leg umpire considers that a bowler is throwing, what should he do?

7. If a bowler goes through his usual bowling action but fails to release the ball - and then "runs out" the batsman who is backing up - what should be the umpire's decision?

8. (a.) How many fielders may be placed on the leg side, backward of square leg?
   (b.) What should an umpire do if this Law is infringed?
   (c) Is it in order for a batsman to mention an infringement to the umpire?

9. Is it the captains or the umpires who decide if play should (a) start (b) stop (c) be interrupted for bad light?

10. If a fielder reaches over the boundary line or rope to make a safe catch, but has his feet clearly inside the boundary - is the batsman out?

11. What is the run out rule when the bails have already been dislodged?

12. is it in order for a fielder to polish the ball?

13. A new batsman can be given "timed out" if he wilfully takes more than how many minutes to come in?

14. A batsman may not hit the ball twice except for what purpose?

15. What must a batsman do before he picks up the ball to toss it back to a fielder?

16. If an umpire miscounts the number of balls in an over - what happens?

17. What signals does an umpire convey when:
    (i) Touching a raised knee with the hand?
    (ii) Extending one arm horizontally?

18. Is it possible for a batsman to be run out from a wide ball?

19. Is it possible to be run out off a no ball?

20. Can a batsman be given out lbw if the ball is padded away outside the line of the off stump?

Answers on page 65.

QUIZ 7

CRICKET TACTICS.

Where possible, it helps if all members of the team understand and agree basic tactics. However, there are times when a captain or a coach may decide to keep certain plans to themselves. It is a fascinating balance to get everything working perfectly - and no-one ever gets it right all the time.

So, what do YOU suggest?

You have been appointed captain, (or senior player) and we need your views... Questions like these confront a captain every game.

1. As the HOME team captain - what information do you require before a match...?

2. As the AWAY team captain - what additional requirements do you have?

3. We field first. What do you require/expect of your team before you take the field?

4. We bat first. What is the Captain's role?

5. In an evening 25 Overs game - do you choose to bat or field first?
   Explain your reasoning.

6. What is your basic field setting? Explain.

7. What tactics can you employ to keep a strong batsman from scoring quickly against your side?

8. Do you have any advice about dealing with a left-handed batsman?

9. What advice can you offer if the opposition have one outstanding bowler?

10. What team behaviour or etiquette do you require from your team?

Answers on page 65.

Michael Atherton. England's recent record-breaking captain.

ANSWERS TO QUIZ SECTION

QUIZ 1. NAME THE PLAYERS

Picture 1. **Curtly Ambrose** (West Indies)
Pace bowler of real quality.

Picture 2. **Sir Donald Bradman** (Australia)
"The Don" Perhaps the greatest run-getter of all time? Played his last Test in 1948. Had he scored one more boundary in his career he would have averaged 100 per innings. In 20 years he made 117 centuries - 29 of them in Test matches. He once made 452 not out and six times exceeded 300, not to mention 37 double centuries.

Picture 3. **Sir Garfield Sobers** (West Indies)
My choice as the most complete and best all-round cricketer ever. A brilliant left-hand batsman. At the age of 21 he scored 365 not out v. Pakistan. In 1968 playing for Nottinghamshire v. Glamorgan, he hit 6 sixes off a six-ball over by Malcolm Nash. He was a Test class bowler who could offer quick swing bowling or slow wrist spinners as required. He played in ninety-three Test matches and made 8,032 runs at 57.78 - including 22 centuries. He took 235 wickets and 109 catches. Not only a superb athlete and cricketer, Sir Garfield was, and still is, widely respected as a fine ambassador for the game.

Picture 4. **Ian Botham** (England)
Legendary and sometimes controversial cricketer. For me, he has a firm place as one of the outstanding personalities in modern cricket. On his day, an inspirational and most competitive all rounder and match winner. His 149 at Headingley to help beat the 1981 Australians remains a special performance.

Picture 5. **Allan Donald** (South Africa)
Top wicket-taking pace bowler.

Picture 6. **Shane Warne** (Australia)
Perhaps the best ever spin-bowler?

Picture 7. **Brian Lara** (West Indies)
Appointed captain in 1998. Record breaking batsman...

Picture 8. **Steve Waugh** (Australia)
Outstanding Aussie batsman and a fierce competitor. 7000 test runs already.

QUIZ 2. from page 57
SELECT YOUR TEAMS

Author's note:
*I would be fascinated to see your selections. We could argue and discuss for ages! All "my" players have represented their countries in 'modern times'. No doubt, experts may say that I should have included several of the "all time greats" like **Victor Trumper**, **Hobbs** or **W. G. Grace** - but they played even before my time! Nor have I considered those who have helped me to compile this book but who must surely rank with the top names in this wonderful game.*

My 'modern' England x My Rest of the World XI

My 'modern' England	My Rest of the World XI
1. **Len Hutton**	1. **Sachin Tendulker** (India)
2. **Graham Gooch**	2. **Donald Bradman** (Aus) (Capt)
3. **P.B.H. May** (Capt)	3. **Vivian Richards** (WI)
4. **Dennis Compton**	4. **Brian Lara** (WI)
5. **David Gower**	5. **Steve Waugh** (Aus)
6. **I.T. Botham**	6. **Garfield Sobers** (WI)
7. **Alan Knott** (WK)	7. **Ian Healey** (Aus) (WK)
8. **Fred Trueman**	8. **Malcolm Marshall** (WI)
9. **Jim Laker**	9. **Shane Warne** (Aus)
10. **Frank Tyson**	10. **Allan Donald** (SA)
11. **Brian Statham**	11. **Ray Lindwall** (Aus)

Reserves and/or Replacements.
[I am only permitted to select three, but any of the following would enhance their teams.]
Quick/Seam bowlers:

Alec Bedser	**Curtly Ambrose** (WI)
	Joel Garner (WI)
John Snow	**Richard Hadlee** (NZ)
	Dennis Lillee (Aus)

Slow bowlers:

J. Embury - Off spin	**Richie Benaud** (Aus)
Tony Lock - Left arm	**Mushtaq Ahmed** (Pak) -

Batsmen:

G. Boycott - Opening bat	**Sunhil Gavaskar** (Ind) -
Alec Stewart - Keeper/batsman	
	Mark Waugh (Aus) No 4 bat.
Godfrey Evans - Keeper	

QUIZ 3. From page 58
MOSTLY ABOUT BATTING.

1.(i) A batsman fails to ground his bat or cross the popping crease to complete a run. The umpire will signal 'one short'. (ii) Backing up (when batting): As the bowler releases the ball, the non-striker should be on the move…This is known as 'backing up'. (when fielding): if a fielder throws at the stumps for a run-out attempt, another fielder should always be 'backing up' behind the stumps to prevent overthrow runs…

2. (i) A short pitched ball which is easy to hit.
   (ii) A ball pitched up towards the batsman so that he can easily strike it in the meat of his bat.

3. (iii) It may vary - but (ii) is recommended.

4. The non-striker, who can see where the ball is.

5. To bring the batsman in line and to get his balance right…

6. The top hand.

7. Turn the wrists to keep the ball down.

8. Gentle hands - let the ball come - don't try to force it away.

9. Yes - to guard his wicket.

10. The one who is running towards the removed bails.

11. Give the batsman out - for wilful obstruction.

12. 2 minutes is permitted.

13. 2 = middle and leg.

14. The batsman should move away and make no attempt to play the ball.

15. Opens the batting and bats all through his side's innings.

16. (i) yes (ii) yes (iii) yes (iv) no. But nb. The umpire's decision is final.

17. Not if the umpire has given him out.

18. In exceptional circumstances the fielding captain may seek permission of the umpire to withdraw an appeal. The umpire will make the final decision.

19. See page 32.

20. My choice would be Sir Donald Bradman. I'm reliably informed that he was the "best ever"…I would like to see for myself.

QUIZ 4. From page 59
MOSTLY ABOUT BOWLING.

1. Part of the front foot must be on or inside the popping crease. page 20

2. See pp17, 22, 23.

3. No - the ball pitched outside the leg stump.

4. Yes. But in "friendly" cricket, it is usual for the umpire to give one warning.

5. If one side is rough and the other side smooth/polished - the ball may swing.

6. Yes.

7. No. He must inform the umpire who will inform the batsman.

8. Usually, the umpire will give a warning, then a final warning. After that a bowler will be barred from bowling again during the innings.

9. Yes.

10. (i) head-high full-toss which a batsman cannot avoid. (ii) a ball which pitches right up close to the batsman and gets underneath his bat.

11. Many reasons but control, rhythm, accuracy all come into it. See page 17.

12. page 26.

13. Grass is not cut really close. Favours the seam bowlers.

14. The bowling arm is close to the line of the stumps. Lbw's are more likely.

15. An off-break bowled with a leg-break hand action. See page 27.

16. It depends on the individual. Side on is recommended. page 18.

17. Bowling so that the batsman is forced to play to your fielders.

18. Set a special field - and bowl to it. Keep the ball on a good length.

19. Extends one arm horizontally.

20. Sir Garfield Sobers (the West Indies all-rounder). He could bowl left arm pace or spin with equal rhythm and success.

QUIZ 5. From page 64
WICKET-KEEPING & FIELDING

1. Slip

2. Point

3. Cover Point

4. Extra Cover

5. Mid-off

6. Fine Leg

7. Third Man

8. Square Leg

9. Mid Wicket

10. Mid On.

11. Stay down until the ball pitches. Don't go too early. page 49

12. Moving into place to cover a wild throw at the stumps.

13. No set rule. Whatever is most likely to help your team.

14. Move quickly. Be still for the catch. Eye on the ball.

15. pages 48 and 49.
16. 5 on the side you expect the ball to be played. 4 on the other side.
17. New ball/away swing bowler/
18. When wickets no longer matter and the run-chase is more important.
19. To soften the blows from the ball/ to allow a tighter fit of the gloves.
20. The captain should call a name. Failing that - one fielder should call "My ball".

QUIZ 6. from page 61
THE LAWS

1. 5 runs.
2. a and d. See diagrams on page 20.
3. No.
4. No
5. He may have a free hit.
6. No ball should be called.
7. Not out. The umpire should call "dead ball".
8. a) No more than 2. b) No ball called. c) Yes.
9. a, b & c: the umpires.
10. Yes.
11. A stump must also be removed from the ground.
12. Yes provided that such polishing wastes no time and that no artificial substance is used.
13. 2.
14. the sole purpose of guarding his wicket
15. ask permission of a fielder.
16. the Umpires count stands.
17. (i) leg bye (ii) no ball.
18. yes.
19. yes.
20. yes. - if the ball would have hit the wicket and there is no attempt to play the ball with the bat.

Quiz 7. From page 64.
CRICKET TACTICS.

These are my answers. You may well have other ideas…

1. The more information your coach/captain knows about the opposition team, your own players, local conditions etc. the better. If the opponents have a useful bowler/batsman – you may wish to say if there is a particular plan to deal with them. You certainly need to know if any of your bowlers is feeling under the weather…

2. At an AWAY game, I like to "walk the playing area" with the entire team before we go in to change. Try to familiarise yourselves with the conditions as much as possible.

3. If we are fielding first, I want a full team meeting in the changing room (with everyone changed) – followed by a proper loosen/warm up outside. Opening bowlers will work together to get themselves fully prepared to bowl. Fielders will sharpen up with some catching/moving… Mental preparation should have started ages ago but this is an important time for a few quiet, purposeful words.

4. If we bat first, and particularly with an inexperienced team, a captain must keep a finger on the pulse. He needs to be available when a wicket falls in order to pass instructions to the next batsmen. Individual batsmen will learn to make decisions but young players will need to know whether to "play steady" or to "push the score along".

5. We bat first – while the light is good. Unless you have a better idea…

6. Call "No Ball".

7. Let him take a single. Get him away from the strike and then keep the weaker batsmen at the striker's end. Young players need help to understand this but it can make a huge difference to a 20 Overs game…

8. Left handers tend to play wider down towards fine leg. Move your fielder wider. If you have an orthodox off spinner or In swinger (ie – moving the ball away from the left hander's legs) give them a thought.

9. The captain leads onto the field/ off the field. Applaud good play. Applaud new batsman onto the field. Applaud opposition team off the field at the end. Thank officials. Team turn-out comes under etiquette. Players should be smart. Avoid sledging.

10. Decide which batsman has the best technique to "manage" their good bowler. It may be a question of simply surviving against him and then raising the run rate against the weaker bowlers.

KNOW THE LAWS

There are some forty-two Laws of the Game - many with sub-sections. Two of the easily misunderstood Laws are outlined below.

Law 36 - Leg before wicket.

Out lbw.

a. Striker attempting to play the ball.

The striker shall be out lbw if he first intercepts with any part of his person, dress or equipment a fair ball which would have hit the wicket and which has not previously touched his bat or a hand holding the bat, provided that:

(i). the ball pitched, in a straight line between wicket and wicket or on the off side of the Striker's wicket, or was intercepted full pitch; and

(ii). the point of impact is in a straight line between wicket and wicket, even if above the level of the bails.

b. Striker making no attempt to play the ball.

The striker shall be out lbw even if the ball is intercepted outside the line of the off-stump, if, in the opinion of the Umpire, he has made no genuine attempt to play the ball with his bat, but has intercepted the ball with some part of his person.

(*Author's note. Unsporting or absurd appeals should be discouraged. However, an important part of the game involves the "appeal" and a well-positioned fielder (ie. keeper, bowler, slip) who believes a batsman to be out LBW must be allowed to appeal to the umpire.)

Law 24 - No ball + diagram on page 19

1. Mode of Delivery.

The umpire shall indicate to the striker whether the bowler intends to bowl over or round the wicket, overarm or underarm, or right or left-handed. Failure on the part of the bowler to indicate in advance a change in his mode of delivery is unfair and the umpire shall call and signal a 'no ball'.

2. Fair Delivery - The Arm.

For a delivery to be fair the ball must be bowled not thrown. If either umpire is not entirely satisfied with the absolute fairness of a delivery in this respect he shall call and signal 'no ball' instantly upon delivery.

3. Fair Delivery - The Feet.

The umpire at the bowler's wicket must be satisfied that in the delivery stride (a) the bowler's back foot has landed within and not touching the return crease or its forward extension, or (b.) some part of the front foot, whether grounded or raised, was behind the popping crease.

4. Bowler attempting to run out non-striker before delivery.

(* Author's note: The Law states that a bowler may run-out the non-striker batsman if he leaves his crease too early. In friendly games, the bowler will ask the umpire to issue one warning to the batsman. If a bowler fails to release the ball, the umpire will rule "dead ball".)

5. Infringement of Laws by a wicket-keeper or a fieldsman.

Law 40. 1. (Wicket-keeper position)

The wicket-keeper shall remain wholly behind the wicket until the ball touches bat or batsman or passes the wicket...or until the striker attempts a run. The umpire at the striker's end will indicate a no ball.

Law 41. 2. (Limitation of on-side fieldsmen)

The number of on-side fieldsmen behind the popping crease at the instant of the bowler's delivery shall not exceed two.

Law 41. 3. (Position of fieldsmen)

(*Author's note: Safety rules must be enforced.)

Recommendations for junior cricket (England and Wales Cricket Board 1998)

It is recommended that no fielder who is under 15 years of age shall be allowed to field nearer than 8 yards in front of the stumps until the batsman has played the ball. For under 13 players, the recommended distance is 11 yards.

6. Runs from a no ball.

The Striker may hit a no ball and whatever runs result shall be added to his score. Runs made otherwise from a no ball shall be scored no balls.

7. Out from a no ball.

Either batsman can be run out from a no ball; also if they break Law 34 (Hit the ball twice), Law 33 (Handled the ball), Law 37 (Obstructing the field).

(*Author's note. **Today's Young Cricketers** includes a sound understanding of **The Laws**. You are strongly encouraged to obtain a copy and to take time out to study them. As Umpire David Shepherd recommends at the start of Chapter 7: "I cannot over-emphasise the need for young players to begin to understand the Laws and to realise how much this will help their game...")

Copies of the most recent edition of **The Laws of Cricket** - with full notes and explanations - can be obtained from: **MCC, Lord's Cricket Ground, London, NW8 8QN.**

INDEX OF NAMES AND CRICKET TERMS

ALL TIME GREAT PLAYERS

Drawn by Peter Hooper.

INTERNATIONAL ACTION PHOTOGRAPHS

By Philip Brown:

THREE USEFUL ADDRESSES

**1) The England and Wales
Cricket Board
ECB
Lord's Cricket Ground
London NW8 8QZ**

**Telephone:
Lord's Cricket Ground:
0171 432 1200
Coaching Department:
0171 440 1748**

For information about all aspects of cricket development - contact the ECB.
All promising young players and coaches should try to attend at least one of the official coaching courses run by the ECB. These courses are organised throughout the country and cater for all ages and all standards. A phone call to the coaching number above will offer helpful advice and put you in touch with the people in your area who can help…

**2) The Lord's Taverners
22 Queen Anne's Gate
London
SW1H 9AA**

Telephone: 0171 222 0707

The Lord's Taverners is a unique Club and Charity. Every year they raise over one million pounds to help young people, and to provide clubs with much needed equipment. They make an important contribution in supporting young people with special needs. For information or assistance or for details about volunteer membership - contact the number shown.

**3) Marylebone Cricket Club
M. C. C.
Lord's Cricket Ground
London NW8 8QZ**

Telephone: 0171 266 2022

Copies of The Laws of Cricket may be obtained from the MCC Book Shop.

TRELOAR TRUST

Registered Charity No. 307103

Education, Independence & Care
for Young People with Disabilities

Incorporating

LORD MAYOR TRELOAR SCHOOL
and
LORD MAYOR TRELOAR NATIONAL SPECIALIST
COLLEGE OF FURTHER EDUCATION

For further information please contact:

TRELOAR TRUST
FROYLE, ALTON, HAMPSHIRE GU34 4JX
Telephone: (01420) 22442

WHEELS FUND
PARK END, ASHTON WALK, WIDEMOUTH BAY, BUDE CORNWALL EX23 0AL
Telephone: (01288) 361562